Japanese Grammar for JLPT N4

Master the Japanese Language Proficiency Test N4

Clay & Yumi Boutwell

INTRODUCTION

Taking the Japanese Language Proficiency Test is a great way to not only assess your Japanese skills, but also to give yourself a concrete goal for your studies.

Goals help increase motivation and motivation makes continuing a difficult task much easier. Also, by making plans to take the test (usually) in a different city, you are making a major investment of time and money. There are few pressures in life that can motivate better than time or money.

HOW TO USE THIS BOOK

This book covers some particles, grammatical patterns, grammar concepts, and special words with grammatical functions. Every entry includes an explanation of the concept, how to use it in a sentence, and then several example sentences.

We highly recommend reading each example sentence several times—even dozens of times. This is hard work, but use the literal translation to help understand how we came up with the more natural English translation.

Learning isolated vocabulary may be useful, but learning vocabulary within a natural context (sentence) while absorbing how the grammar works boosts understanding. While you read this book (paperback, tablet, or computer), you may want to use your smartphone to play the sound files.

SOUND FILES

While you read an example sentence (many times), listen to it. This will help with memorization. We also recommend "shadowing" the text. Listen to the Japanese and then repeat it out loud. After that, try to speak with the speaker. Pay attention to the pronunciation of individual words and the intonation of the whole sentence.

The download link at the end of this book includes sound files for all the grammar points and their example sentences.

ABOUT CLAY & YUMI

Yumi was a popular radio DJ in Japan for over ten years. She has extensive training in standard Japanese pronunciation which makes her perfect for creating these language instructional audio files.

Clay has been a passionate learner of Japanese for over twenty years now. He started what became his free language learning website, www.TheJapanesePage.com, way back in 1999 as a sort of diary of what he was learning.

In 2002, he and Yumi began TheJapanShop.com as a way to help students of Japanese get hard-to-find Japanese books. Since then, they have written many books on various Japanese language topics.

Yumi and I are **very grateful** for your purchase and we truly hope this book will help you improve your Japanese. **We love our customers and don't take a single one of you for granted.** If you have any questions about this book or Japanese in general, I invite you to contact us below by email or on social media.

Clay & Yumi Boutwell (and Makoto & Megumi) in Fukui, Japan
clay@thejapanshop.com

@theJapanShop

https://www.facebook.com/LearningJapaneseatTheJapanShop

https://www.TheJapanShop.com

https://www.MakotoPlus.com

あとで

MEANING:

■ afterwards; after; after this; later

HOW TO USE:

■ Verb (past form) + あとで + (what comes after)

↳ 食べた**あとで**、寝た。 **After** (I) ate, I slept. (casual)

■ Noun + の + あとで

↳ 学校の**あとで**、買い物をします。 **After** school, I'll go shopping.

STUDY NOTES:

■ It is sometimes written with the kanji 後で.

EXAMPLES:

今は忙しいので、**あとで**電話します。

now | as for | busy | therefore | **later** | to make a phone call

I'm busy now, so I'll call **later**.

あとで、ゆっくり話しましょう。

later | unhurriedly | let's speak

7

Let's catch up later.

■ あと - the で can be omitted in casual speech.

↳ 仕事の<u>あと</u>、飲みに行かない？ **After** work, wanna go get a drink?

宿題<u>のあとで</u>ゲームしよう！

After homework, let's play a (video) game!

[宿題 (homework); ゲーム (video game); しよう (let's)]

～ば／～れば

MEANING:

■ if A then B; conditional expression

HOW TO USE:

There are many variations depending on the type of word. Read through the usages below closely, and then memorize one or two examples, found on the next page, of each type.

■ **-u Verbs:** Change the "u" to "e" + ば

↳ Example: 話す hanas**u** → hana**se** + ば → 話**せ**ば (if someone talks)

■ **-ru Verbs:** stem + れば

↳ Example: 食べる tabe~~ru~~ → 食べ + れば → 食べれば (if someone eats)

■ **-i Adjectives:** stem (minus the final い) + ければ

↳ Example: 小さ~~い~~ → 小さ + ければ → 小さ**ければ**

■ **-na Adjectives & Nouns:** -na Adjective (without the -na) or Noun + なら（ば） or であれば

↳ -na Adjective Example: 静かならば (if quiet) or 静かであれば (if quiet)

↳ Noun Example: 車ならば (if car) or 車であれば (if car)

9

■ **irregular verbs:**

↳ する (to do) → すれば (if someone does)

↳ くる (to come) → くれば (if someone comes)

<u>STUDY NOTES:</u>

■ This grammar point may be difficult due to the many conjugations, but if you memorize a few examples from each group and try to use them in conversation, it will eventually become second nature to you.

■ For -na adjectives and nouns, the final ば is often omitted: 静<small>しず</small>かなら (if quiet) or 電車<small>でんしゃ</small>なら (if a train)

<u>EXAMPLES:</u>

■ -u Verbs:

- 話<small>はな</small>す → 話<small>はな</small>せば (if someone speaks)
- 行<small>い</small>く → 行<small>い</small>けば (if someone goes)
- 読<small>よ</small>む → 読<small>よ</small>めば (if someone reads)

■ -ru Verbs:

- 食<small>た</small>べる → 食<small>た</small>べれば (if someone eats)
- 飲<small>の</small>める → 飲<small>の</small>めれば (if someone drinks)
- 寝<small>ね</small>る → 寝<small>ね</small>れば (if someone sleeps)

■ -i Adjectives:

- 小<small>ちい</small>さい → 小<small>ちい</small>さければ (if small)

- 大^{おお}きい → 大^{おお}きければ (if large)
- 忙^{いそが}しい → 忙^{いそが}しければ (if busy)

■ -na Adjectives & Nouns
- 静^{しず}かな → 静^{しず}かならば (if quiet) or 静^{しず}かであれば (if quiet)
- 車^{くるま} → 車^{くるま}ならば (if car) or 車^{くるま}であれば (if car)

■ irregular verbs:
- する → すれば (if someone does)
- くる → くれば (if someone comes)

And a few example sentences:

読^よ**めば**分^わかる。
read | **if** | understand
If you read (it), (you'll) understand.

車^{くるま}で行^いけ**ば**、はやい。
car | by | to go | **if** | fast
If you go by car, it's fast.

薬^{くすり}を飲^のめ**ば**、治^{なお}る。
medicine | (direct object marker) | drink | **if** | heal
If you take the medicine, you'll get better.

11

明日天気がよければ、海に行きましょう。

tomorrow | weather | **if** good | ocean | to | let's go

If the weather is good tomorrow, let's go to the beach!

NEGATIVE:

The negative "if" is made as follows:

Verb stem	+ なければ
-i adjective + く	+ なければ
-na Adjective / Nouns + で	+ なければ

先生に聞か**なければ**、分かりません。

teacher | to | ask | **if not** | won't understand

If you do**n't** ask the teacher, you won't understand.

勉強し**なければ**、試験に落ちる。

study | **if don't** | test | to | fail (fall)

If you do**n't** study, you'll fail the test.

いい天気で**なければ**、ピクニックに行けません。

good | weather | **if not** | picnic | can't go

If the weather is**n't** good, we can't go on a picnic.

～ばいいですか

■ how; why; when; what should

HOW TO USE:

■ Verb (ば form) + (change the ending of the last mora from an "u" to an "e") + ばいい

  ↳ する → (change the "u" to "e") →すれ+ばいい: どうすれ**ばいいですか**？ (**What should** I do?)

STUDY NOTES:

■ This is used to seek instructions from someone.

EXAMPLES:

さいふを落（お）としたんですが、どうすれ**ばいいです**
か。

wallet | (direct object marker) | dropped | (explainer) | but | in what way | **would be good | (question)**
I dropped my wallet. **What should I do**?

この本（ほん）はいつ返（かえ）せ**ばいいですか**。

this | book | as for | when | return | **would be good |**
(question)
When **should** I return this book?

13

場合

MEANING:

■ In the case of; in the event of

HOW TO USE:

■ Verb (dictionary form) + 場合
　　　　　　　　　　　　　　ば あ い

■ Noun + の + 場合
　　　　　　　ば あ い

■ -na Adjectives + な + 場合
　　　　　　　　　　　ば あ い

■ -i Adjectives + 場合
　　　　　　　　ば あ い

STUDY NOTES:

■ Usually, 場合 is followed by the topic marker は.
　　　　　　ば あ い

EXAMPLES:

非常の場合、このボタンを押してください。
ひ じょう　ば あ い　　　　　　　　　　お

emergency | (limiter; 's) | **situation** | this | button |
(direct object marker) | press | please
In case of emergency, press this button.

お金がない場合は、アルバイトしてください。
かね　　　ば あ い

money | not | **situation** | as for | part-time job | please do
If you don't have money, then get a job!

14

ことができる

MEANING:

■ can; able to

HOW TO USE:

■ Verb (dictionary form) + ことができる

　↳ 食^たべる (to eat) → 食^たべることができる (can eat; able to eat)

STUDY NOTES:

■ This is another way to express the potential (can do) form. 食^たべ<u>られる</u> = 食^たべ<u>ることができる</u>

■ The polite form is (dictionary form verb) + ことができます

■ The negative (cannot do) is (dictionary form verb) + ことができない or ことができません

■ The kanji is 出^で来^きる which is literally, "go out and come."

星は夜に見る<u>ことができる</u>。

stars | as for | night | at | to see | **able to**

Stars **can** be seen at night.

友だちは日本語を上手に話す<u>ことができます</u>。

friend | as for | Japanese language | (direct object) |
skillfully | to speak | **able to**

My friend **can** speak Japanese well.

～だす（出す）

MEANING:

■ suddenly; to start; to burst into

HOW TO USE:

■ Verb (-masu stem) + だす

STUDY NOTES:

■ Often used with adverbs such as 急<small>きゅう</small>に (suddenly) or 突然<small>とつぜん</small> (all of a sudden)

EXAMPLES:

急<small>きゅう</small>に雨<small>あめ</small>が降<small>ふ</small>り<u>出<small>だ</small>した</u>。

suddenly | rain | fall | **started to**

It suddenly **started** to rain.

突然<small>とつぜん</small>、その子<small>こ</small>は道路<small>どうろ</small>に飛<small>と</small>び<u>出<small>だ</small>した</u>。

Suddenly | that | child | as for | road | into | jumped | **burst out**

Suddenly, that child ran **out** into the street.

お酒<small>さけ</small>に酔<small>よ</small>った彼女<small>かのじょ</small>は急<small>きゅう</small>に泣<small>な</small>き<u>出<small>だ</small>した</u>。

sake | with | drunk | she | as for | suddenly | crying | **started to**

Drunk with alcohol, she suddenly **began** to cry.

17

できるだけ

MEANING:

■ as much as possible

HOW TO USE:

■ Adverbial expression; use as you would, "as much as possible."

STUDY NOTES:

■ It is made of できる (can; able to) + だけ (only)

EXAMPLES:

ここはうるさいので、**できるだけ**大^{おお}きい声^{こえ}で話^{はな}し
てください

here | as for | loud | therefore | **as much as possible** |
big | voice | with | please speak
It's loud here, so please speak as loudly **as you can**.

ここは図書館^{としょかん}なので、**できるだけ**静^{しず}かにしてくだ
さい。

here | as for | library | therefore | **as much as possible**
| quietly | please do
This is a library, so please be as quiet **as possible**.

どうも

- truly; really; very much

- I'm not sure

- Used to stress the meaning of a sentence or to show doubt.

- Mainly used with ありがとう and すみません.

- Often, どうもありがとう is shortened to just どうも. A variant is saying どうも twice – どうもどうも

Meaning #1: truly; really; very much:

<u>どうも</u>ありがとうございます。
<u>**very much**</u> | thanks (polite)
Thank you <u>**very**</u> much.

19

うちの子がお世話になったそうで、**どうも**すみま
せん。

our | child | aid | became | appears to have | **very** |
sorry
I want to thank you for **troubling** to help our child.

Meaning #2: not sure; doubtful

どうもわかりませんので、もう一度言ってくださ
い。

very-not sure-not understand-therefore-more-one-
time-speak-please
I **simply** don't get it. Could you say it one more time?

～始める（始める）

MEANING:

■ begin to

HOW TO USE:

■ Verb (-masu form) – ます + はじめる

STUDY NOTES:

■ This is used to show a continuous action, operation, natural phenomeon, or practice that has a beginning and end.

EXAMPLES:

急きゅうに雨あめが降ふり**始はじめた**。

suddenly | rain | fall | **started**
It suddenly **started** raining

春はるが来きて、桜さくらが咲さき**始はじめました**。

spring | came and | cherry blossoms | bloom | **began**
Spring has come and the cherry blossoms **have begun** to bloom.

21

先週からこの学校に通い**始めました**。

last week | from | this | school | to | commuting |
began

(I) **started** attending this school last week.

～はずだ

MEANING:

- It must be; it should be; it is expected that; ought to

HOW TO USE:

- Verb (dictionary form) + はずだ
- Noun + の + はずだ
- -na Adjective + な + はずだ
- -i Adjective + はずだ

STUDY NOTES:

- This is also はずです (です is polite of だ)

EXAMPLES:

クレイさんはアメリカ人だから、英語が分かる**はずです**。

Clay (honorific) | as for | an American person |
therefore | English language | to understand | **ought to**
Since Clay is an American, he **should** understand
English.

23

この穴の中に一億円が隠してある**はずです**。

this | hole | midst of | in | hundred million | concealed | **ought to**

This hole is **supposed** to have a hundred million yen hidden inside.

〜はずがない

MEANING:

■ Hardly possible that; it couldn't be the case that; cannot be

HOW TO USE:

■ Verb (dictionary form) + はずがない

■ Noun + の + はずがない

■ -na Adjective + な + はずがない

■ -i Adjective + はずがない

STUDY NOTES:

■ Use this to strongly emphasize the impossibility of something. This is used when someone encounters a situation that seems to contradict a fact or strongly held belief.

EXAMPLES:

日本語能力試験N1が簡単な**はずがない**。

JLPT | N1 | (subject marker) | easy | **ought to be | isn't**
There's no way the JLPT N1 is easy.

この時計がこんなに安い**はずがない**。偽物だよ。

this | watch | (subject marker) | such an extent |

inexpensive | **ought to be | isn't** | fake | is | (emphatic)

This watch **can't be** this cheap. It's a fake.

あの人が独身の**はずがない**わ。昨日奥さんに会っ
たわよ。

that | person | (subject marker) | single | **ought to be |
isn't** | (feminine ender) | yesterday | (other person's)
wife | to | met | (emphasis)

There's no way that guy is single. I met his wife
yesterday.

〜かどうか

MEANING:

■ Whether or not; I don't know if...

HOW TO USE:

■ Plain form of a verb, adjective, or noun + かどうか

STUDY NOTES:

■ The format is: (A) + かどうか + (B)
Where (A) shows some condition or state and (B)
usually shows doubt often with: わかりません (don't
know) or other words showing doubt or negativity:

- 決めていません (not settled)
- 覚えていません (don't remember)
- 忘れました (forgot)

キャンプに行<u>く**かどうか**</u> まだ決めていません。

camp | to | to go | **whether or not** | as of yet | not decided

I haven't decided **if** I'm going to camp **or not**.

あのコンピューターは便利<u>**かどうか**</u>わからない。

that | computer | as for | useful | **whether or not** | don't know

I don't know **whether or not** that computer is useful.

〜かもしれない

MEANING:

- It's possible that; it might be; perhaps; possibly; may

HOW TO USE:

- plain form verb/noun/adjective + かもしれない

STUDY NOTES:

- Other forms: かも (casual) / かもしれません (more formal)

EXAMPLES:

彼は明日 私 の家に来る**かもしれません**。

he | as for | tomorrow | my | house | to | to come
perhaps

__It's possible__ he will come to my house tomorrow.

明日は雪が降る**かもしれません**。

tomorrow | as for | snow | to fall (snow) | **might**

It **may** snow tomorrow.

〜に気がつく

MEANING:

■ to notice; to realize; to become aware

HOW TO USE:

■ Verb (casual) + こと + に気がつく

■ Noun + に気がつく

STUDY NOTES:

■ This is often said in the past: I realized (past tense):
に気がついた

EXAMPLES:

コンビニで財布を持っていないこと**に気がつい**
た。

convenience store | at | wallet | (direct object) | don't
have | **realized**

I was in a convenience store and **realized** I didn't have
my wallet.

私は彼女がそこにいた**ことに気がつかなかった**。

I | as for | she | there | exists; there | **didn't realized**
that

I **didn't realize** that she was there.

～ことにする

MEANING:

- Decide to do~; decide on

HOW TO USE:

- Verb (dictionary form) + ことにする

STUDY NOTES:

- This shows a decision made with one's will. I decided that...

- The more polite form is ことにします.

- For continuing actions, ことにしている or ことにしています

EXAMPLES:

今日からもっと日本語を勉強することにします。

now | from | more | Japanese langauge | (direct object marker) | to study | **decide to**

I **decided to** study Japanese more from today.

夕食後に本を読むことにします。

supper | after | book | (direct object marker) | to read | **decide upon**

I**'ll** read a book after supper.

～ことになる

MEANING:

■ has been decided that...; has been arranged so that

HOW TO USE:

■ Verb (dictionary form) + ことになる

STUDY NOTES:

■ ことになる expresses a decision that has been made irrespective of one's desire. This stands in contrast to the previous ことにする which shows a decision made by oneself.

■ The causer of the arrangements is not specified, making ことになる similar to the passive.

■ Since it is a usually expressing a decision already made, this is usually in the past: ことになった

■ ことにする and ことになる can be confusing, but ことにする shows the speaker's will and ことになる shows a decision was made potentially outside the speaker's will. To illustrate this, consider the following examples:

私は会社を辞めることにしました。

I decided to leave the company.

私は会社を辞めることになりました。

It was decided that I leave the company.

<ruby>私<rt>わたし</rt></ruby> は<ruby>来月結婚<rt>らいげつけっこん</rt></ruby>する<u>**ことになりました**</u>。

as for me | next month | to marry | **has been decided**

I am **getting** married next month.

<ruby>山田<rt>やまだ</rt></ruby>さんはパーティーで<ruby>司会<rt>しかい</rt></ruby>をする<u>**ことになりま**</u>

<u>**した**</u>。

Mr. Yamada | as for | party | at | host | (direct object
marker) | to do | **has been decided**

Mr. Yamada **will be** the host for the party.

33

〜く／ 〜にする

MEANING:

■ To make something ~; to choose to do

HOW TO USE:

■ -na Adjective + にする

↳ 大切 (important): 大切にする (to take good care of; to cherish)

■ -i Adjective − い + にする

↳ 安い (cheap): 安くする (to make (something) less expensive; to lower the price)

STUDY NOTES:

■ While the form is different between -na and -I adjectives, the meaning is the same. It makes what the adjective describes happen.

EXAMPLES:

この本は大切にします。

this | book | cherish | **will do**
I'**ll** treasure this book.

もうちょっと安くしてくれない？

more | a little | cheaper | **to do** | won't you?
Can you **make** it a little cheaper?

34

まま

MEANING:

■ Without change; doesn't change; continuing the same state

HOW TO USE:

■ Noun + の + まま

↳ 靴のまま (keeping shoes on)

■ Verb (past/た form) + まま

↳ 靴をはいたまま (still wearing shoes)

■ Verb (negative ない form) + まま

↳ 靴をはかないまま (still not wearing shoes)

■ -na Adjectives + な + まま

↳ 不便なまま (still inconvenient)

■ -i Adjectives + まま

↳ あたたかいまま (still warm)

STUDY NOTES:

■ You'll hear this all the time with demonstratives:

↳ このまま | そのまま | あのまま

These all mean "as it is," "as things are," or "without change." Basically the この expresses ideas and objects that are near the speaker, その are for things or ideas nearby, and あの are for distant objects or thoughts.

Another somewhat idiomatic usage is the word: わがまま (selfish; egoist) which literally means "oneself + without change."

EXAMPLES:

窓を開けた**まま**にしておいてください。

window | (direct object marker) | opened | **as is** | leave | please

Please **keep** the windows open.

少しの間、その**まま**でお願いします。

a little | span of time | **as is** | with | please

Please stay **as you are** for a little bit.

この問題は未解決の**まま**です。

This | problem | (direct object marker) | not solved | **as is** | is

This issue **remains** unresolved.

まだ〜ていない

MEANING:

■ not yet

HOW TO USE:

■ Verb (て form) + ていない

↳ まだ食^たべていない (not eaten yet)

STUDY NOTES:

■ The ていない is often shortened to てない in speech.

EXAMPLES:

まだ宿題^{しゅくだい}が終^{おわ}っていません。
not yet | homework | **not** finished
I haven't finished my homework **yet**.

まだ漢字^{かんじ}は全部覚^{ぜんぶおぼ}えていない。
not yet | kanji | as for | all | remember | **not**
I **still** don't know all the kanji.

37

または

MEANING:

■ or; either... or... [choice between A or B]

HOW TO USE:

■ Noun + または + Noun

↳ コーヒー**または**お茶 coffee **or** tea

STUDY NOTES:

■ Use when offering a choice between two or more options. This is a somewhat formal way to express "or."

■ If there are more than two options, the first options are usually marked with か or nothing at all: りんご、オレンジ、**または**ぶどう apples, oranges, **or** grapes

EXAMPLES:

鉛筆、**または**ペンで答えをマークしてください。

pencil | **or** | pen | with | answer | (direct object marker) | mark | do | please

Mark your answers in pencil **or** pen.

うどん、そば、**または**ラーメンが選べます。

udon | soba | **or** | raman | can choose

Can choose between udon, soba, **or** ramen.

〜みたい

MEANING:

■ seems; looks like; similar to

HOW TO USE:

■ Verb (dictionary form) + みたい

　↳ 風邪をひいたみたい seems (I've) caught a cold

■ Noun + みたい

　↳ うそみたい unbelievable [literally, seems like a lie]

■ -na or -I Adjectives + みたい

　↳ 大丈夫みたい looks okay

　↳ 安いみたい looks inexpensive

STUDY NOTES:

■ This is used to show speculation about certain things or facts and is a colloquial form of ようだ (see the entry in this book)

■ Adding a に makes this into an adverbial phrase (add before a verb to describe that action): バカみたいに見える (to appear foolish)

あの人は日本人**みたい**ですね。

that | person | as for | Japanese person | **it seems** |
isn't it

That person **seems** to be Japanese.

風邪をひいた**みたい**。

cold | (direct object marker) | caught | **it seems**

It seems (I) caught a cold.

今日は暑くて夏が来た**みたい**です。

Today | as for | hot | summer | came | **seems like**

Today is hot and **seems like** summer has come.

40

〜ながら

MEANING:

■ while; during

HOW TO USE:

■ Verb (-masu stem form) + ながら

↳ 食_たべます (to eat) → 食_たべ → 食_たべながら (while eating)s

STUDY NOTES:

■ This construction shows two actions are being performed at the same time.

■ Some grammatical patterns are easy to construct. Simply take the stem of a -masu form of a verb and add ながら to mean "while (doing verb)."

EXAMPLES:

ポップコーンを食_たべ**ながら**、映画_{えいが}を見_みました。

popcorn | (direct object marker) | eat | **while** | movie | (direct object marker) | saw

(I) ate popcorn **while** watching a movie.

歩_{ある}き**ながら**、友達_{ともだち}と話_{はな}しました。

walking | **while** | friend | with | spoke

While walking, I talked to a friend.

41

〜ないで

■ Don't; without doing

■ Verb (negative ない form) +で

↳ 食べないで don't eat

■ ないで is used both to show something is not done and also as a command or suggestion to not do something.

窓から手を出さ**ないで**。

window | from | hand | (direct object marker) | thrust out | **don't**

Don't stick your hand out the window.

昨日は、夕食を食べ**ないで**、寝ました。

yesterday | as for | supper | (direct object) | not eating | slept

Last night, I went to sleep **without** eating supper.

42

〜ないでおく

MEANING:

■ deliberately refrain from ~ in order to ~

HOW TO USE:

■ Verb (negative ない form) +で

↳ 言(い)わないでおく refrain from speaking (so a secret won't be revealed, for example)

STUDY NOTES:

■ Adding the おく after the negative 〜ないで implies some deliberate action (or refraining from some action) to achieve some purpose.

EXAMPLES:

今日(きょう)は血液検査(けつえきけんさ)があるので、朝(あさ)ごはんは食(た)べ**ない**
でおく。

today | as for | blood test | exists | therefore |
breakfast | as for | **not** eat
I have a blood test today, so I'm **not going to** eat
breakfast.

これは深刻な問題なので、子供には話さ**ないでお**
こう。

this | as for | serious | problem | therefore | children |
to | as for | speak | **not**

This is a serious matter, so let**'s not** talk about it with our
kids.

日本語を忘れ**ないでおく**ために、毎日勉強しよ
う。

Japanese language | (direct object marker) | **don't**
forget | **in advance** | in order to | every day | study |
let's

Let's study Japanese everyday so we won**'t** forget it!

〜なくてもいい（不必要）

MEANING:

■ Don't have to; not necessary

HOW TO USE:

■ Verb (negative plain form) ＋なくても｜いい

　↳食(た)べなくてもいい (you) don't have to eat

STUDY NOTES:

■ This is used to show some action is unnecessary.

EXAMPLES:

今日(きょう)は日曜日(にちようび)なので、学校(がっこう)に行(い)か**なくてもいい**です。

today | as for | Sunday | therefore | school | to | **don't have to** go

Today is Sunday so you **don't have to** go to school.

ここは洋室(ようしつ)なので、靴(くつ)を脱(ぬ)が**なくてもいい**。

here | as for | Western style room | therefore | shoes | (direct object marker) | remove | **don't have to**

This is a Western-style room, so you **don't have to** take off your shoes.

45

〜なくてはならない

MEANING:

■ Must do; have to do

HOW TO USE:

■ Verb (negative plain stem form) ＋なくてはならない

↳ 勉強^{べんきょう}しなくてはならない (I) have to study

STUDY NOTES:

■ This is used for necessities and obligations and often about oneself.

EXAMPLES:

高速道路^{こうそくどうろ}では制限速度^{せいげんそくど}を守^{まも}ら**なくてはならない**。

highway | on | as for | speed limit | **must keep**
On highways, the speed limit **must be observed**.

日本^{にほん}に住^すむなら、日本^{にほん}の法律^{ほうりつ}を守^{まも}ら**なくてはならない**。

Japan | in | live | if | Japanese | law | (direct object marker) | **must** obey
If you live in Japan, you **must** obey Japanese laws.

大学に合格したいなら、しっかり勉強し**なくては**
ならない。

university | for | pass | want to | if | well | study | **must do**

If you want to get into college (by passing the entrance exam), you **have to** study hard.

なら

MEANING:

■ if; in the case of

HOW TO USE:

■ Verb (dictionary form) + なら

↳ 食べるなら if (you will) eat

■ Noun + なら

↳ あなたなら if it's you (we're talking about)

■ -na and -i Adjective +なら

↳ 静かなら if quiet

STUDY NOTES:

■ This is often used to give one's advice or opinion based on a conditional.

あなた**なら**、できます。 **If** it's you (we are talking about), you can do it.

日本人**なら**、そういうことはしない。

Japanese person | **if** | such a thing | don't do
A Japanese person wouldn't do such a thing.

仕事する**なら**、早くして。

work | to do | **if** | hurry up | do
If you have to get work done, hurry up and do it.

好きな花**なら**、買います。

like | flower | (subject marker) | pretty | **if** | to buy
If I like the flower, I'll buy it.

〜なさい

■ do this; command to do something

■ Verb (-masu stem form) + なさい

  ↳ ピーマンを食べなさい (eat your green peppers)

■ This can be either a firm or gentle command. This is often heard by mothers asking or ordering their children to do something.

私の質問に答え**なさい**。

my | question | for | answer **(command)**
Answer my question.

毎日、歯を磨き**なさい**。

every day | tooth | (direct object marker) | polish
(command)
Brush your teeth every day.

〜にくい

MEANING:

■ difficult to do; hard to do

HOW TO USE:

■ Verb (-masu stem) + にくい

↳ 読みにくい (**hard** to read)

STUDY NOTES:

■ にくい follows the same pattern as やすい (easy to) which is also found in this collection.

EXAMPLES:

この字は読みにくい。

this | character | as for | to read | **difficult to**
This character is **hard** to read.

彼は答えにくい質問をした。

he | as for | answer | **difficult to** | question | did
He asked an awkward (**difficult** to answer) question.

〜のですか・んですか

■ for emphasis and explanation or seeking an explanation

HOW TO USE:

■ -na Adjective / Noun (only with questions) + な + のですか or な + んですか

  ↳ 先生<u>なんです</u> ((I am) a teacher)

■ -i Adjective + のですか or んですか

  ↳ いい<u>んですか？</u> ((Are you) sure it's okay?)

■ Verb (plain form) + のですか or んですか

  ↳ 行く<u>んですか？</u> ((Are you) going?)

STUDY NOTES:

■ The んです form is the casual form which is often used in conversational Japanese. It is used for emphasis while still offering an explanation or a request for one.

EXAMPLES:

何かあった<u>んですか</u>？警察が来てますが。

something | happened | **(question)** | police | are here |

52

(softener)
What's going on? The police are here.

実は、昨日の夜、泥棒に入られた**んです**。

actually | yesterday's | night | robber | by | was
entered | **(explanation)**
Actually, we were robbed last night.

こんな夜中に何をしている**んですか**？

such a | middle of night | during | what | doing |
(question explanation)
What are you doing here at this time of night?

〜のは〜だ

MEANING:

■ regarding ... is ...; for giving an explanation, reason, or emphasis

HOW TO USE:

■ -na Adjective / Noun + な + のは〜だ (or です)

■ -i Adjective + + のは〜だ (or です)

■ Verb (plain form) + のは〜だ (or です)

STUDY NOTES:

■ What follows は shows a reason or close relationship with the topic (は).

EXAMPLES:

日本語の文法を勉強する<u>のは</u>、たいへん<u>だ</u>。
Japanese (language) | grammar | (direct object marker)
| to study | **regarding** | hard work | **is**
Learning Japanese grammar is hard work.

私に日本語を教えてくれた**のは**、佐藤先生**です**。

me | to | Japanese (language) | (direct object marker) |
teach and | gave | **regarding** | Satou | teacher | **is**

It was Ms. Sato who taught me Japanese.

私が信じている**のは**、神様だけ**だ**。

I | believing | **regarding** | God | only | **is**

All I believe in is God.

〜のような

MEANING:

■ Like; similar to

HOW TO USE:

■ Noun + の + ような + (noun/noun phrase)

↳ 雪のような白い髪 (snow-**like** white hair)

STUDY NOTES:

■ The な makes this (like; similar to) into an adjective which describes an object.

EXAMPLES:

人生は旅のようなものだ。

life | as for | travel | **like** | thing | is

Life is **like** a journey.

彼は今日いつものような元気がない。

he | as for | today | always | **like** | energetic | don't have

He isn't himself today.

～のように

MEANING:

■ Like; similar to

HOW TO USE:

■ Noun + の + ように

↳ 風_{かぜ}のように走_{はし}る (run like the wind)

STUDY NOTES:

■ The に makes this (like; similar to) into an adverb which describes the action. It is often used with metaphors like the above "like the wind"

EXAMPLES:

彼_{かれ}のように歌_{うた}いたい。

him | **like** | sing | want to
I want to sing **like** him.

彼_{かれ}は子_こどものように笑_{わら}った。

he | as for | child | **like** | laughed
He laughed **like** a child.

のに

MEANING:

■ to do (something); for the purpose of doing (something); in the process of doing (something); in order to

HOW TO USE:

■ Verb (dictionary form) + のに

↳ 話^{はな}すのに (in order to talk)

STUDY NOTES:

■ Be careful to not confuse this with the more common のに meaning of "although" or "even though."

EXAMPLES:

カレーを作^{つく}る**のに**、何^{なに}がいりますか？

curry | (direct object marker) | to make | **process of doing** | what | need | (question marker)

What do you need **to** make curry?

この本^{ほん}を読^よむ**のに**、一^{いっ}ヶ月^{げつ}かかりました。

this | book | (direct object marker) | to read | **in order to** | one month's time | spent

It took me a month to read this book.

58

お～ください

MEANING:

■ please do (honorific)

HOW TO USE:

■ お + Verb (-masu stem form) + ください

　↳ お読みください (please read)

■ お or ご + (する) Actionable Nouns + ください

　↳ ご遠慮ください (please refrain (from doing something))

STUDY NOTES:

■ This is a polite way to ask someone to do something. On use with nouns that imply action (する nouns).

EXAMPLES:

ここに名前をお書きください。

here | at | name | (direct object marker) | **(polite)** | write | **please**

Please write your name here.

しばらくここでお待ちください。

short while | here | at | **(polite)** | wait | **please**

Please wait here for a while.

59

～られる

MEANING:

■ potential form; can; ability to do something

HOW TO USE:

■ -ru Verbs (drop the る) + られる

↳ 食べる (to eat) → 食べ → 食べ<u>られる</u> (able to eat)

■ -u Verbs (change the "u" sound to "e") + る

↳ 飲む (to drink) → (む becomes め) → 飲<u>める</u> (able to drink)

↳ 話す (to speak) → (す becomes せ) → 話<u>せる</u> (able to speak)

■ Irregular Verbs:

↳ する (to do) → できる (able to do; can)

↳ くる (to come) → こられる (able to come)

↳ やる (to do) → やれる (able to do; can)

STUDY NOTES:

■ The rules for forming verbs with this grammar point

60

can be confusing. Familiarize yourself with the basic rules and then learn many examples. Eventually, it will become second-nature.

■ With the potential, が often marks the object: 漢字を読む (to read kanji) becomes 漢字が読める (able to read kanji)

EXAMPLES:

あの子はネギが食べられます。

that | child | as for | green onions | **able to** eat

That child **can** eat green onions.

彼女は五つの言語が話せます。

she | as for | five | (connector) | language | **able to** speak

She **can** speak five languages.

〜させる

MEANING:

■ make someone do something; causative form (from the viewpoint of the person making someone else do something)

HOW TO USE:

■ -ru Verbs + させる

↳ 食べる→食べさせる (to make someone eat)

■ -u Verbs (ない form) + せる

↳ 飲む→飲まない→飲ませる (to make someone drink)

STUDY NOTES:

■ 〜させる is from the **viewpoint of someone making someone else (marked with に) do something (the "perpetrator")**. The *next entry* is from the **viewpoint of the person made to do something (the "victim")**.

■ The irregular forms are:

する→させる

くる→こさせる

やる→やらせる

62

先生は宿題をやり直させた。
せんせい　しゅくだい　　　　　なお

teacher | as for | homework | (direct object) | redo | **made (me)**

My teacher **made** me redo my homework.

お母さんは娘に部屋を掃除させました。
かあ　　　むすめ　へや　　そうじ

mother | as for | daughter | to | room | (direct object marker) | clean | **made her**

The mother **made** her daughter clean her room.

[This is from the **viewpoint of the person making someone else do something (the "perpetrator")**. The は shows who did the forcing and the に shows who was forced.]

〜させられる

MEANING:

■ to be made to do something; causative passive form (from the **viewpoint of the person made to do something (the "victim")**)

HOW TO USE:

■ -ru Verbs (dictionary form) + drop the る + させられる

  ↳食べさせられる made to eat (something)

■ -u Verbs (dictionary form) + drop the "u" and change it into an "a" sound + せられる

  ↳飲む → む becomes ま → 飲ませられる made to drink (something) (this is often shortened to 飲まされる in speech)

■ Irregular Verbs:

  ↳する (to do) → させられる (forced to do)

  ↳くる (to come) → こさせられる (forced to come)

  ↳やる (to do) → やらせられる (forced to do)

■ This is from the **viewpoint of the person made to do something (the "victim")**. 〜させる is from the **viewpoint of someone making someone else (marked with に) do something (the "perpetrator")**.

■ This is a combination of two important verb forms: The "make someone do something" (causative form させる) and the "have done something" (passive form （ら）れる)

EXAMPLES:

子どもはお母さんに薬を飲ま**せられた**。

mother | as for | child | to | medicine | (direct object marker) | **forced** to drink

The mother **made** the child take the medicine.

[Note: in spoken Japanese, 飲まされた is often used. This is from the viewpoint of the person being made to do something. The は shows who was forced and the に shows who did the forcing.]

私は先生に勉強さ**せられた**。

I | as for | teacher | from | study | **was made to**

The teacher **made** me study.

65

This and the previous entry is a little confusing, so let's compare the two.

Sentence #1: (させる) Viewpoint (marked by は) of the person forcing someone else to do something (the "perpetrator"):

先生は私に宿題をやり直<u>させた</u>。

teacher | as for | me | to | homework | (direct object) | redo | **made (me)**

My teacher **made** me redo my homework.

Sentence #2: (させられる) Viewpoint (marked by は) of the person forced to do something (the "victim"):

私は先生に宿題をやり直<u>させられた</u>。

I | **as for** | teacher | **by** | homework | (direct object) | redo | **was made (to do)**

I **was made** to do homework **by** my teacher.

The trick is to realize the first sentence (させる) is from the **viewpoint of the person making someone else do something** and the second sentence (させられる) is from the **viewpoint of the person being made to do something**.

〜せいで

MEANING:

■ on account of; because of

HOW TO USE:

■ Verb (dictionary form) + せいで

　↳ 食べたせいで (due to have eaten)

■ Noun + の + せいで

　↳ 猫のせいで (because of the cat)

■ -na Adjectives + な + せいで

　↳ 静かなせいで (because it was quiet)

■ -i Adjectives + せいで

　↳ 悪いせいで (because it was bad)

STUDY NOTES:

■ This is often used in a negative light. To say "thanks to" or "because of" in a positive light, use おかげで.

台風の**せいで**電車が止まった。

typhoon | **on account of** | train | stopped
The train was stopped **because of** a typhoon.

病気の**せいで**、彼は会社を辞めなければならなかった。

sickness | **due to** | he | as for | company | (direct object marker) | quit | had to
Due to his illness, he had to leave the firm.

～し

MEANING:

■ also; and; what's more...

HOW TO USE:

■ Verb (dictionary form) + し

↳ お金<ruby>金<rt>かね</rt></ruby>がないし、時間<ruby>時間<rt>じかん</rt></ruby>もないし ((I) have no money and (I) have no time)

■ Noun + だ + し

↳ 電話<ruby>電話<rt>でんわ</rt></ruby>だし、カメラだし (phone and (also) a camera)

■ -na Adjective + だ + し

↳ 静<ruby>静<rt>しず</rt></ruby>かだし (it's quiet and)

■ -i Adjectives + し

↳ 優<ruby>優<rt>やさ</rt></ruby>しいし (kind and)

STUDY NOTES:

■ This form of connecting actions, ideas, or things is often used when giving a reason for doing or not doing something.

69

恵<ruby>めぐみ</ruby>さんは、優<ruby>やさ</ruby>しい<u>し</u>、かわいい<u>し</u>、頭<ruby>あたま</ruby>がいい<u>し</u>、人気者<ruby>にんきしゃ</ruby>です。

Megumi | kind **and** | cute **and** | head is good **and** | popular person | is

Megumi is kind **and** cute **and** smart **and** popular.

最近<ruby>さいきん</ruby>のスマートフォンは電話<ruby>でんわ</ruby>だ<u>し</u>、カメラだ<u>し</u>、メールもできる<u>し</u>、とても便利<ruby>べんり</ruby>です。

recent | smartphones | as for | phone **and** | camera **and** | e-mail | can do **and** | very | convenient | is

Smartphones these days are phones, cameras, **and** they can e-mail. They are very convenient.

そうだ

■ Looks like; appears to be; seems to be

■ Verb (-masu stem form) + そうだ (or そうです)

↳ 遅れそうだ (it seems (I) will be late)

■ -na Adjective + そうだ (or そうです)

↳ 静かそう (seems quiet)

■ Verb (-masu stem form) + そうだ (or そうです)

↳ おいしそう (it looks delicious)

■ そうだ or そうです can also mean "I heard that."
We'll cover that usage in the next entry.

71

EXAMPLES:

今日は、いい天気になり**そうだ**。

today | as for | good | weather | will become | **it seems**

It's going to be a beautiful day.

しまった。会社に遅れ**そうだ**。

darn | office | to | late | **it looks like**

Sheesh. I'm going to be late for work.

〜そうだ

MEANING:

■ I heard that; it is said that

HOW TO USE:

■ Verb (dictionary form) + そうだ (or そうです)

↳ やめるそうだ (I heard (someone will) quit)

■ Noun / -na Adjectives + だ + そうだ (or そうです)

↳ 日本人だそうです (I heard (someone) is Japanese)

■ -i Adjectives + そうだ (or そうです)

↳ このテストはむずかしいそうだ I heard the test
is difficult

STUDY NOTES:

■ The previous entry covers そうです as meaning "it
looks like." This usage relays second-hand information.

この店はおいしい料理がある**そうです**。

this | store | as for | delicious | food | exists | **I heard that**

I heard this store has delicious food.

ニュースによると、さっき九州で地震があった

そうだ。

news | according to | recently | Kyushu | at |
earthquake | existed | **I heard**

According to the news, there was an earthquake in Kyushu earlier.

天気予報によると、明日は雨が降る**そうだ**。

weather forecast | according to | tomorrow | as for |
rain | to fall | **I heard**

The weather forecast says it's going to rain tomorrow.

すぎる

MEANING:

■ too much; excessive; to overdo something

HOW TO USE:

■ Verb (-masu stem) + すぎる (or すぎます)

↳ 言_いいます (to speak) → 言_いい → 言_いいすぎる (to say too much)

■ -na Adjectives + すぎる (or すぎます)

↳ 簡単_{かんたん} (easy; simple) → 簡単_{かんたん}すぎる (too easy)

■ -i Adjectives + drop the い + すぎる (or すぎます)

↳ 暑_{あつ}い (hot) → 暑 → 暑_{あつ}すぎる (too hot)

STUDY NOTES:

■ The kanji is 過_すぎる which means "to exceed" but it is most often written in kana only.

■ To show a negative degree or something lacking using ない, the form is なさすぎる:

常識_{じょうしき}が**なさすぎる** not enough common sense

遠慮_{えんりょ}が**なさすぎる** not enough discretion; not reserved enough

75

昨日の夜は宴会があったので食べ**過ぎました**。

yesterday's | night | as for | banquet | there was |
therefore | to eat | **too much**

There was a banquet last night and I ate **too much**.

この宿題は難し**すぎる**。

this | homework | as for | difficult | **too much**

This homework is **too** difficult.

〜たばかり

MEANING:

■ just finished (doing something)

HOW TO USE:

■ Verb (past form) + ばかり

　↳ 勉強_{べんきょう}したばかり (just studied)

STUDY NOTES:

■ Add ばかり to the past (た) form of a verb to indicate something just finished or just occurred.

EXAMPLES:

映画_{えいが}は始_{はじ}まっ**たばかり**だ。

movie | as for | started | **just** | (copula)
The movie **just** started.

起_おき**たばかり**なので、まだ眠_{ねむ}いです。

woke up | **just** | therefore | still | sleepy | am
I **just** woke up and so I'm still sleepy.

〜たがる

MEANING:

■ wants to do; seems eager to do; appears to be anxious about

HOW TO USE:

■ Verb (たい (to want) form) + minus い + がる

↳ 行きたがる (eager to go)

STUDY NOTES:

■ To say "I want" (to do something), use the たい form of a verb. This form たがる is used to describe someone else's desires.

■ These forms are also used: がらない (don't want); がっている (is wanting); がった (wanted)

■ Make the "to want" たい form of a verb, drop the い, and add がる: 食べます (to eat) → 食べたい → 食べたがる (seems to want to eat)

■ Don't use this form with those socially above (teacher, elders, etc.)

78

彼女<ruby>か<rt></rt></ruby>はもう帰りた**がっている**。

she | as for | already | return home | **seems to be wanting**

She **seems to want** to go home already.

犬はこのブランドの餌を食べた**がらない**。

Dog | as for | this | brand |of | (dog) feed | (direct object marker) | **doesn't seem to want** to eat

The dog **doesn't seem to want** to eat this brand of food.

〜たら

MEANING:

■ After; when; if

HOW TO USE:

■ Verb (past form) + ら

   ↳ 食^たべる (to eat) → 食^たべ<u>た</u> (ate) → 食^たべ<u>たら</u>

■ Noun + だったら (だった + ら)

   ↳ 日本^{にほん}だっ<u>たら</u> (if Japan)

■ -na Adjective + だったら (だった + ら)

   ↳ きれいだっ<u>たら</u> (if pretty)

■ -i Adjectives + drop い + かった

   ↳ 新^{あたら}し<u>かったら</u> (if new)

STUDY NOTES:

■ This conditional usually means "if" but it can also mean "after" as in "after this, comes that." The first three examples on the next page illustrate this.

晩ごはんを食べたら、寝ます。

dinner | eat | **after** | to sleep
After (I) eat dinner, I'll go to sleep.

夏休みになったら、日本に帰ります。

summer vacation | **after** | Japan | to | return
I will return to Japan **after** the summer vacation.

ご飯を食べたら、薬を飲んでください。

meal | (direct object marker) | to eat | **after** | medicine
| (direct object marker) | drink | please
After you eat your meal, take your medicine.

お酒を飲んだら、眠くなります。

alcohol | (direct object marker) | drink | **if** | sleepy |
become
If I drink alcohol, I'll become sleepy.

～たらどうですか

MEANING:

■ why don't you?

HOW TO USE:

■ Verb (past た form) + らどう（ですか）

↳ 勉強<ruby>勉強<rt>べんきょう</rt></ruby>したらどうですか？ (why don't you study?)

STUDY NOTES:

■ Use this form when giving advice. Just because it is in the た form doesn't mean it implies the past tense.

EXAMPLES:

<ruby>学校<rt>がっこう</rt></ruby>に<ruby>行<rt>い</rt></ruby>っ<u>たらどうですか</u>？

school | to | go | **how about**
Why don't you go to school?

ちょっと<ruby>休<rt>やす</rt></ruby>ん<u>だらどう</u>？

A little | rest | **how about**
Why don't you rest a bit?

<ruby>分<rt>わ</rt></ruby>からなかったら、<ruby>先生<rt>せんせい</rt></ruby>に<ruby>聞<rt>き</rt></ruby>い<u>たらどう</u>？

Don't know | if | teacher | to | ask | **how about**
If you don't get it, **why not** ask the teacher?

82

〜てあげる

MEANING:

■ to do a favor for

HOW TO USE:

■ Verb (て form) + あげる

  ↳ やってあげる ((I'll) do it for you)

STUDY NOTES:

■ Other forms: あげた (past); あげない (negative); あげます (polite)

■ Use this form to say you are doing something for someone else or someone is doing something for someone else.

EXAMPLES:

ちょっとお金を貸してあげる。

a little | money | (direct object marker) | loan | **give**

I'**ll** lend you some money.

正しいやり方を見せてあげます。

correct | way of doing | (direct object marker) | to show | **give**

I'**ll** show you the correct way to do it.

～ているあいだに～

MEANING:

- while; during the time between

HOW TO USE:

- Verb (ている form) + 間（あいだ）に
  - ↳ 待（ま）っている間（あいだ）に (while waiting)

STUDY NOTES:

- It is either written in kana or with the kanji 間（あいだ）. This form is used to show the speaker/writer intentionally does something during an interval of time.

EXAMPLES:

眠（ねむ）っ**ている間（あいだ）に**財布（さいふ）を盗（ぬす）まれた。

sleeping | **while** | wallet | (direct object marker) | was stolen

My wallet was stolen **while** I was sleeping.

電話（でんわ）を**している間（あいだ）に**泥棒（どろぼう）が入（はい）った。

phone | (direct object marker) | doing | **during** | thief | entered

While (I) was on the phone, a thief broke in.

84

〜ていただけませんか

MEANING:

■ Could you please (polite)

HOW TO USE:

■ Verb (て form) + いただけませんか

STUDY NOTES:

■ This is a polite form to ask someone to do something. いただけません means something like "won't you accept ...?"

EXAMPLES:

ちょっと待って<u>いただけませんか</u>？

a little | wait | **won't you accept** | (question marker)
Would you please wait a little?

もっとゆっくり話して<u>いただけませんか</u>？

more | slowly | speaking | **won't you accept** |
(question marker)
Would you mind speaking more slowly?

〜てくれる

MEANING:

■ please do; please do a favor; would you mind

HOW TO USE:

■ Verb (て form) + くれる

　↳ 教^{おし}えてくれますか (please teach me)

STUDY NOTES:

■ This is used to either ask someone to do something for you (would you mind ... ?) or to express the fact that someone did something for you or someone else.

■ The negative くれませんか is often used for politeness. And the shortened くれ version is used in casual speech with a feel of a command.

詳しい話を聞かせて<u>**くれます**</u>か？

detailed | story | let me listen | **<u>give me</u>** | (question)

Can you **give** me more details?

ちょっと静かにして<u>**くれる**</u>？

A little | be quiet and | **<u>give me</u>**

Can you be quiet for a second?

〜てくれてありがとう

MEANING:

■ Thank you for doing...

HOW TO USE:

■ Verb (て form) + くれてありがとう（ございま
す）

↳ 見せてくれてありがとう (thanks for showing me)

STUDY NOTES:

■ Use this to express gratitude when someone does
something for you. You can add ございます for
politeness.

EXAMPLES:

日本語を教えてくれてありがとうございます。

Japanese language | teach | received | **thank you**
Thank you for teaching me Japanese.

引っ越しを手伝ってくれてありがとう。

moving | helped | received | **thank you**
Thanks for helping me move.

〜てみる

MEANING:

■ try to do; try and

HOW TO USE:

■ Verb (て form) + みる

↳ 食べてみる (to try and eat)

STUDY NOTES:

■ This is usually said when trying something new, kind of like the English, "I'll (verb) and see" or "I'll give (verb) a go."

■ The polite みます form is also used. To say, "I'd like to try to do…" use 〜てみたい

一回やって**てみる**。

one time | try **and** | **see**

I'll give it one **try**.

このケーキを食べ**てみます**。

this | cake | (direct object marker) | eat and | **see**

I'll **try** this cake.

このドレスを着**てみて**もいいですか？

this | dress | (direct object marker) | wear | **try** | good
| is it

May I **try** on this dress?

富士山に登っ**てみたい**。

Mt. Fuji | on | climb and | **like to try**

I'**d like** to climb Mt. Fuji.

And the negative form to mean "if (I) don't try…"

実際に使っ**てみない**と、分からない。

actual use | use and | **not try** | don't understand

Unless I actually use it, I won't get it.

〜てもらう

■ to have someone do something for you

HOW TO USE:

■ Verb (て form) + もらう

　↳ 来_きてもらう (to have someone come)

STUDY NOTES:

■ The polite -masu form as well as the negative forms are often used. Use this when you receive some help from someone else.

■ Also see 〜てあげる (to do something for someone) in this collection.

EXAMPLES:

医者_{いしゃ}に診_みてもらいました。

doctor | by | see/consult | **received**
I saw the doctor.

お巡_{まわ}りさんに駅_{えき}への行_いき方_{かた}を教_{おし}えてもらった。

police officer | by | train station | to | 's | way to go |
(direct object marker) | instructed | **received**
A police officer gave me directions to the train station.

91

～ておく

MEANING:

■ Do something in advance; leave (something in its current state)

HOW TO USE:

■ Verb (て form) + おく

↳ お金をためておく (save up money)

STUDY NOTES:

■ This is also used with the -masu form ～ておきます and in the -te form ～ておいて

EXAMPLES:

災害に備えてトイレットペーパーを買っ**ておく**。

disaster | for | make preparations for | toilet paper | (direct object marker) | buy | **in advance**

Stock **up** on toilet paper in case of a disaster.

泥棒が入らないように、鍵をかけ**ておいて**ください。

robber | (subject marker) | not enter | in order that | lock | (direct object marker) | to lock and | **leave as** | please

Please lock the door to prevent burglars from entering.

〜てくる・〜ていく

MEANING:

■ has become

HOW TO USE:

■ Verb (て form) + くる

STUDY NOTES:

■ This V て + くる describes a situation that is continually changing from the past to the present (from the speaker's point of view)

■ V て + いく is for an action that will continue to change from the present (speaker's point of view) to the future.

EXAMPLES:

日本語のレッスンがだんだん 難 しくなって**きた**。

Japanese language | 's | lesson | increasingly | difficult | be**came to be**

Japanese lessons are getting harder and harder.

94

インターネットのおかげで、人々の生活は変わっ**てきた**。

internet | due to | peoples' | lives | as for | changed | u

The Internet has changed people's lives.

これからは、電気自動車がもっと増え**ていく**だろう。

here | from | electric | car | more | increase | **come to be** | I suppose

We will see more electric cars in the future.

〜てくる #2

MEANING:

■ to go do (something) and come back; to start something

HOW TO USE:

■ Verb (て form) + くる

↳ 店_{みせ}に行_いってくる (to run to the store)

STUDY NOTES:

■ This describes leaving somewhere temporarily for a trivial purpose.

EXAMPLES:

近_{ちか}くのコンビニでお茶_{ちゃ}を買_かって**きます**。

nearby | convenience store | at | tea| (direct object marker) | buy **and come**

I'll get some tea at a nearby convenience store.

お弁当を食べる前に、手を洗ってくるね。

lunch box | (direct object marker) | to eat | before |
hand | (direct object marker) | wash **and come** |
(emphatic)

I'm going to go wash my hands before eating my lunch.

家まで忘れ物を取りに行ってくる。

house | until | forgotten thing | (direct object marker) |
to get | for the purpose of | go **and come**

I'm gonna go home and pick up some things I forgot.

～てしまう

MEANING:

■ completed; ended up; feeling of regret

HOW TO USE:

■ Verb (て form) + しまう（polite: しまいます or
past: しまった）

　↳全部食べてしまった (ate all of it)

■ Verb (て form) + minus the て + ちゃう（casual
speech; past: ちゃった）

　↳全部食べちゃった (ate all of it)

STUDY NOTES:

■ This expresses a completion of some act or indicates
something was done by accident. This usually, but not
always, implies some regret.

■ The ちゃう becomes じゃう in some informal cases
and after some sounds.

宿題を忘れ**てしまった**。

homework | (direct object marker) | forget and |
completely
I **totally** forgot to do my homework.

映画館で寝**ちゃった**。

movie theater | at | sleep | **completely**
I fell asleep at the movie theater.

先に宿題をやっ**てしまった**らどう？

before | homework | (direct object marker) | do and |
complete | how about?
Why don't you just get your homework **over with**?

〜てすみません

MEANING:

■ I'm sorry for...

HOW TO USE:

■ Verb (て form) + すみません

↳ 遅れてすみません (sorry for being late)

STUDY NOTES:

■ This is fairly straightforward. Say what you are sorry for, end the verb in the て form, and add すみません.

EXAMPLES:

コップを割ってしまっ**てすみません**。

glass cup | (direct object marker) | unfortunately broke and | sorry

Sorry I broke the glass cup.

先日、失礼なことを言っ**てすみません**でした。

the other day | rude | thing | saying and | **sorry**

Sorry for being rude the other day.

〜てよかった

MEANING:

- I'm glad that

HOW TO USE:

- Verb (て form) + よかった

  ↳ 買^かってよかった (glad I bought)

STUDY NOTES:

- Use this form when you want to say "I'm glad (I)..."

EXAMPLES:

無事^{ぶ じ}に帰^{かえ}って**てよかった**。

without incident | returned and | **it's good**
I'm glad you arrived safely.

電車^{でんしゃ}に間^まに合^あって**てよかった**。

train| for | in time | **it's good**
I'm glad (I) made the train in time.

101

〜ても・〜でも

MEANING:

■ even; even though

HOW TO USE:

■ Verb (て form) + も

　↳ 話_{はな}しても (even if (you) speak)

■ Noun / -na Adjectives + でも

　↳ お金_{かね}でも (even money)

　↳ 静_{しず}かでも (even silence)

■ -i Adjectives + minus い + くても

　↳ 新_{あたら}しくても (even if (it's) new)

STUDY NOTES:

■ The noun and -na adjective forms use でも.

子ども**でも**わかるはずです。

child | **even** | understand | ought to | (copula)
Even a child ought to know.

いくらお金をもらっ**ても**悪いことはできない。

however much | money | receive | **even** | bad thing |
can't do
No matter how much you pay, I won't do evil.

どんなに安く**ても**、ニセモノは買いたくない。

However | cheap | **even** | fake | as for | buy | don't
want to
Even if it's cheap, I don't want to buy a fake.

と

MEANING:

■ upon; whenever A happens, B then happens

HOW TO USE:

■ Verb (dictionary form) + と

↳ 起きると (upon waking)

STUDY NOTES:

■ Don't confuse this with the conjunction と (and).
This is used to show a cause and effect connection
between two things or ideas.

EXAMPLES:

ピザを食べすぎると太ります。

pizza | (direct object marker) | to eat too much | **upon
doing so** | become fat
I gain weight **when** I eat too much pizza.

あなたに会うと嬉しくなります。

you| to | to meet | **upon doing so** | happy | become
I'm happy **when** I meet you.

～という～

MEANING:

■ called; named; such a

HOW TO USE:

■ Noun (or phrase) + という

STUDY NOTES:

■ It is sometimes written with the kanji: と言う which is made of the quotation marker と and 言う (to speak). This can be 「てっいう」 in casual conversation.

EXAMPLES:

「マロ」<u>という</u>犬を飼っています。

Maro | **such a** | dog | (direct object marker) | keeping
I have a dog **named** "Maro."

昔、彦一さん<u>という</u>面白い人がいました。

long ago | Hikoichi | **called** | interesting | person |
(subject marker) | there was
Long ago, there was an interesting person **called**
Hikoichi.

つづける（続ける）

MEANING:

■ keep on; go on and on

HOW TO USE:

■ Verb (-masu stem) + つづける

STUDY NOTES:

■ The kanji is 続ける.

EXAMPLES:

三年間、日本語を勉強し続けました。

three years time | Japanese language | (direct object marker) | study | to do | **continued**

I've **continued** to study Japanese for three years.

そのお姫様は百年間眠り続けました。

that | princess | as for | a hundred years span | sleeping | **continued**

That princess has **continued** to sleep for a hundred years.

メロスは一日中走り続けました。

Melos | as for | all day long | run | **continued**
Melos **continued** to run all day long.

[Melos is from a famous short story by Dazai Osamu.
Click here for the story read by Yumi designed to help
you fall asleep: https://thejapanesepage.com/sleep/#t-
1638911425986]

～は～が

■ as for ~ has ~

HOW TO USE:

■ Takes up a topic (A) followed by a condition or nature of that topic (B) and how it is described (C).

A は B が C

象<ruby>は<rt>ぞう</rt></ruby>鼻<ruby>が<rt>はな</rt></ruby>長<ruby>い<rt>なが</rt></ruby>

象**は**鼻**が**長い

Elephant **は** nose **が** long

Elephants have long noses.

STUDY NOTES:

■ The が and what follows describes the は topic.

EXAMPLES:

私<ruby><rt>わたし</rt></ruby>のお父さん**は**背<ruby><rt>せ</rt></ruby>**が**高<ruby><rt>たか</rt></ruby>いです。

my | father | **as for** | height | tall | is

My dad is tall.

私<ruby><rt>わたし</rt></ruby>の家<ruby><rt>いえ</rt></ruby>**は**庭<ruby><rt>にわ</rt></ruby>**が**広<ruby><rt>ひろ</rt></ruby>い。

my | house | **as for** | yard | wide

My house has a big yard.

〜やすい

MEANING:

■ easy; not difficult; prone to (do something)

HOW TO USE:

■ Verb (-masu stem form) + やすい

　↳ わかります (to understand) → わかり<u>やすい</u>
(**easy to** understand)

STUDY NOTES:

■ This is formed just as you would にくい (difficult to)
but means the opposite.

■ In addition to meaning "easy to" it can also mean
"prone to" or "likely to happen" as in: この 車 は事故
が起こりやすい。 An accident is likely to happen with
this car.

EXAMPLES:

大きい字のほうが読み<u>やすい</u>。
big | letter | is more | to read | **easy to**
Big letters are **easier to** read.

～よう（だ）

MEANING:

■ It seems; I heard that; I saw that (something appears to be so after using the five senses)

■ like (metaphor)

HOW TO USE:

■ Verb (plain form) + よう（だ）

　↳怒っているようだ (appears to be angry)

■ Noun + の + よう（だ）

　↳雪のようだ (it looks like snow)

■ -na Adjectives + な + よう（だ）

　↳好きなようだ (appears to like)

■ -i Adjectives + よう（だ）

　↳高いようだ (seems expensive)

STUDY NOTES:

■ This is also used with demonstratives such as そのようだ (it seems that way)

110

EXAMPLES:

頭 が痛いし、熱があるし、風邪をひいた**ようだ**。

head | hurts and | fever | exists and | cold | caught |
seems

My head hurts and I have a fever. It **seems** I've caught a cold.

Here is the second meaning which is used in a metaphoric sense.

あなたの手は冷たい。まるで氷 の**ようだ**。

your | hand | as for | cold | as if | ice | it seems to be

Your hand is cold as ice.

～ようと思う

MEANING:

■ thinking of doing; planning on

HOW TO USE:

■ Verb (volitional よう form (see below for instructions)) + 思う

↳買う (to buy)→買おう→買おうと思う (thinking of buying)

[Note: while the title of this point starts with よう, it's really "o" + う for -u verbs. See below for instructions.]

STUDY NOTES:

■ The volitional form shows intent or is used to suggest doing something. Here's how to form it:

- **-ru verbs:** drop the る and add よう: 食べる (to eat) → 食べよう (intent to eat; let's eat)

- **-u verbs:** change the final vowel sound to "o" and add a う:
  飲む (to drink) → 飲もう (intent to drink; let's drink)
  買う (to buy)→買おう (intent to buy; let's buy)

- する (to do) →しよう (intent to do/let's do)

- くる (to come) →こよう (intent to come)

112

今日からもっと日本語を勉強<u>しようと思います</u>。

today | from | more | Japanese language | (direct object marker) | study | **thinking about**

I'm **planning to** study Japanese more from now on.

夏休みの間に日本に行<u>こうと思っています</u>。

summer vacation | during | Japan | to | to go | **thinking about**

I'm **thinking of** going to Japan during summer break.

ぜひ

MEANING:

■ by all means; certainly; without fail

HOW TO USE:

■ ぜひ + (what you want to happen)

↳ ぜひ来てください (by all means, please come)

STUDY NOTES:

■ The kanji is 是非.

EXAMPLES:

来週、**ぜひ**うちに遊びに来てね。

next week | **by all means** | house | to | play | for the
purpose of | come | (emphatic)
By all means, come visit us next week!

今度来る時にぜひ連絡してください。

next time | come | time | on | by all means | contact |
do | please
Next time you come, by all means please reach out.

全然～ない

MEANING:

■ (not) at all

HOW TO USE:

■ 全然 + verb (negative ない form)

↳ 全然ダメ (not good at all; total failure)

STUDY NOTES:

■ Use mostly with negative verbs, but recently, in casual speech, it is also used with non-negative verbs as in: 全然いいよ (It's totally fine!).

■ Both the kanji and hiragana only are used.

■ 全然 can also be used to modify adjectives as in our first example below.

あの映画は**全然**面白く**ない**。

that | movie | as for | **at all** | **not** interesting
That movie isn't interesting **in the least**.

お金は**全然ありません**。

money | as for | **at all** | **doesn't exist**
I don't have any money at all.

全然わかりません。

at all | don't understand
I don't understand **at all.**

Useful Counters

Bold and underlined entries indicate an irregular pronunciation.

	人	歳・才	個	本
1	**ひとり**	**いっさい**	**いっこ**	**いっぽん**
2	**ふたり**	にさい	にこ	にほん
3	さんにん	さんさい	さんこ	**さんぼん**
4	**よにん**	よんさい	よんこ	よんほん
5	ごにん	ごさい	ごこ	ごほん
6	ろくにん	ろくさい	**ろっこ**	**ろっぽん**
7	しちにん ななにん	ななさい	ななこ	ななほん
8	はちにん	**はっさい**	**はっこ** はちこ	はちほん
9	きゅうにん くにん	きゅうさい	きゅうこ	きゅうほん
10	じゅうにん	**じゅっさい**	**じゅっこ**	**じゅっぽん**

	枚	匹	冊
1	いちまい	**いっぴき**	**いっさつ**
2	にまい	にひき	にさつ
3	さんまい	**さんびき**	さんさつ
4	よんまい	よんひき	よんさつ
5	ごまい	ごひき	ごさつ
6	ろくまい	**ろっぴき**	ろくさつ
7	ななまい	ななひき しちひき	ななさつ
8	はちまい	**はっぴき**	**はっさつ**
9	きゅうまい	きゅうひき	きゅうさつ
10	じゅうまい	**じゅっぴき**	**じゅっさつ**

📓 To ask, how many, simply add 何 before the
counter: 何人 (なんにん) how many people?; 何枚 (なんまい) how many
sheets (of paper)?

Digital Bundles

Download Link

Please go to this website to download the MP3s for all the Japanese: (There is an exclusive free gift on kanji waiting there too)

http://japanesereaders.com/grammar4

As an extra added bonus, here is a coupon **for 10%** off your next order at www.TheJapanShop.com. Just use the coupon:

MATANE

(Just use the above word in CAPITALS; no minimum order amount!)

Thank you for purchasing and reading this book! To contact the authors, please email them at help@thejapanshop.com. See also the wide selection of materials for learning Japanese at www.TheJapanShop.com and the free site for learning Japanese at www.thejapanesepage.com.

Made in the USA
Monee, IL
14 September 2023